33

.:.

reflections on the
gospel of saint john

For carolyn, grace, and hannah—
It is my joy to walk with you in the eternal love
and abundant life that are in christ jesus.

⁚

In Christian art, the square halo identified a living person presumed to be a saint. Square Halo Books is devoted to publishing works that present contextually sensitive biblical studies, and practical instruction consistent with the Doctrines of the Reformation. The goal of Square Halo Books is to provide materials useful for encouraging and equipping the saints.

©2022 Square Halo Books, Inc.
P.O. Box 18954 | Baltimore, MD 21206
www.SquareHaloBooks.com

ISBN 978-1-941106-27-3
Library of Congress Control Number: 2022941215

Printed in the United States of America

33

reflections on the gospel of saint john

ANDREW ROYCROFT

FOREWORD BY Malcolm Guite
ARTWORK BY Ned Bustard

SQUARE HALO BOOKS

foreword

You hold in your hands a beautiful sequence of poetic meditations on the Gospel of Saint John by one of Northern Ireland's finest new poets. John has of course always been the favourite Gospel for poets and mystics, since every episode, every miracle, or "sign" as John prefers to call them, is teeming with meaning and beauty, with graces and revelations to be dwelt upon afresh by each new generation. T.S. Eliot spoke of poetry as "concentration without elimination," and by choosing the early mediaeval practice of forming a series of thirty-three word poems, a word for each year of Jesus' earthly life, Andrew Roycroft has crafted a series of miniatures, like little prayer beads, or perhaps more like mediaeval illuminations, each of which can both concentrate and expand your contemplation as you sound out its syllables on your tongue and lift its images up to your mind's eye.

Although these poems are in one sense concentrated miniatures, in another sense their purpose is to expand your mind, open your under-standing, help you glimpse the immensity of the mystery disclosed in the gospel. And poetry is just the right art form to do this, for in poetry every word counts, every word is set in careful and tingling relation to every other, opening a reciprocal network of meaning for the reader.

And if the thirty-three words in each poem weave a net to catch meaning and mystery, then the thirty-three poems do the same in relation to each other, from the opening lines of the sequence:

> Into the wordless gap
> sounds the Word made flesh—

To the final reflection that all our words, even all the words of the Gospel itself, cannot entirely contain the mystery of grace in Christ:

> though all in fairest minuscule inscribed—
> they never could contain the sense
> of this eternal Word,
> or capture Christ.

And then, in addition to all this intricately linked poetry, we have the added dimension of Ned Bustard's beautiful linocut prints, which draw on the style and language of the famous Book of Kells, the same world from which Andrew's poetic inspiration also comes. There is a beautiful image to accompany every poem, images inspired not only by the poetry but also by the Gospel passages that in their turn inspired the poem, so that in a sense, there is a kind of Trinitarian exchange: a Gospel begetting a poem and an image proceeding from and informed by both poem and Gospel.

You could read this sequence through in a sitting and that itself is a moving experience, but you can also take it slowly, contemplatively, perhaps over a thirty-three day retreat. The evocative, allusive, haiku-like poetry encourages you to do so, as do the compelling images, made for contemplation. You could easily learn one of these poems at the beginning of the day, fix the accompanying image in your mind, and then take both out with you for a quiet walk, letting poem and image walk with you and teach you new things.

Of course, all of this depends on familiarity with the distinct tone and beauty of John's gospel, and Roycroft has helpfully given the key verse that lies behind each poem after the poem itself, so that, to return to our Trinitarian image, Gospel, poem, and picture can all be at play in your mind at once, can all "co-inhere," as the theologians would say.

There is a particular art to writing biblically inspired poetry. You must avoid the dangers of mere paraphrase on the one hand and infidelity to the spirit of the text on the other. You must let each Bible verse become a seed that grows slowly in your mind, flowering eventually into the poem. Or, to use Paul's terms, you must move constantly from *ta gramma*, the letter, to *ta pneuma*, the Spirit, for "the letter killeth but the Spirit giveth life." I learnt these lessons slowly myself, in writing *Parable and Paradox*, my own poetic sequence on the sayings of Jesus, and it gives me great joy to see a younger poet already mature in the art which it took me so long to learn. So ponder slowly the beautifully inscribed "letter" of this book, and you will find that each poem is full of the spirit, full of life and wisdom.

—MALCOLM GUITE

1

Into the wordless gap
sounds the Word made flesh—
new logic
granting grounds
for hope—
all former words
will now deliver
their long pregnant promise
of a world, once spoken,
finally made fresh.

LOGOS

11

His unstrapped sandals
cast on Jordan's shore,
Christ enters the stream
where before
all Israel
had plunged.
Emerging, shod
with good news,
he is ready to baptise
these lesser men
with heaven's fire.

III

The last-drunk wedding dregs
seem an unlikely place
to set a sign,
but such wine-bloodied waters
will make glad the hearts of all
who taste
the ripe glory of this Vine.

When the wine ran out, the mother of Jesus said to him, "They have no wine." [2:3]

IV

And so this fabric
will come asunder,
yield to deconstruction,
unravel all that was
so skilfully knit in conception;
a frail, torn down house,
whose ruin hints at hope
beyond its tattered veil.

V

This fleshly arm,
mechanism of muscled bone,
pulse and impulse
set in chain,
cannot open a mother's womb
nor heaven's gate;
instead the Rabbi speaks
the wind-borne work
of being born again.

VI

At Jacob's well, Jacob's Son
comes alone, weary for water.
A tarnished bride, midday travel
through adulterous hills
discovers to her
Christ
who, emptying himself, will one day
fill Sychar's sons and daughters.

AND HE HAD TO PASS THROUGH SAMARIA. [4:4]

VII

Seeing the Father, so he, the Son,
per se,
living, will give life;
with words will bring from soiled beds
all
who rising, heed his summoning voice—
to judgement
or to joy
eternal.

VIII

This Loaf King—
whom we would crown just for the crusts
—insists on being Living Bread, granting
life through his flesh and blood, on proving
himself true manna
sent from heaven for us.

IX

Ropes hang slack
from distracted hands,
their arresting grip
now lame.
Held in tension by
these word-woven bands,
their forced confession,
tongues fettered to proclaim,
"No one ever spoke like this man."

THE OFFICERS THEN CAME TO THE CHIEF PRIESTS
AND PHARISEES, WHO SAID TO THEM,
"WHY DID YOU NOT BRING HIM?" [7:45]

X

The old man, adrift
in innumerable sands—
outnumbered
by hope's expanse—
drowns moonwards
in a star ocean.
With nebulous glance,
eyes rejoicing
in the promised Son,
he lipreads,
"Before Abraham was, I AM."

YOUR FATHER ABRAHAM REJOICED THAT HE WOULD SEE MY DAY. HE SAW IT AND WAS GLAD. [8:56]

XI

Tilth eyed,
muddling towards Siloam,
hands cupping refracted rays,
he rinses darkness
out of newborn sight—
once-slackened retinae
now nerved
to perceive
the Light of the World,
unseen
by mud-blind men.

XII

Keeping the wolf from the Door,
the Shepherd calls;
bringing in his own
he shames the unsound staff
of pilfering crooks who came before.
Laying down,
he wrests
a flock into his care.

XIII

A distance out from death Christ
remains,
love's absence
forestalling glory.
If he had been here
a brother need not die,
but he, through tarrying presence
speaks of coming life,
and awakened joy.

XIV

Coming to the kernel of it all,
with earthen words Christ will explain
that this hour at which he
must fall
is harvest-sure
of life to come,
of hope
with the grain.

TRULY, TRULY, I SAY TO YOU, UNLESS A GRAIN OF WHEAT FALLS
INTO THE EARTH AND DIES, IT REMAINS ALONE; BUT IF IT DIES,
IT BEARS MUCH FRUIT. [12:24]

XV

Quitting upper room light,
having a bellyful of broken bread
and the stooping talk
of one who,
new anointed,
washes sinners' feet,
Judas takes his course
through Jerusalem streets,
swallowed whole in night.

XVI

Cocksure, Peter crows
that unlike this brood
he will stay,
will go as far as blood;
but Christ speaks
a denied dawn,
withheld light
which will wring
the breath out of such words.

PETER SAID TO HIM, "LORD, WHY CAN I NOT FOLLOW YOU NOW?
I WILL LAY DOWN MY LIFE FOR YOU." [13:37]

XVII

Mere waste of breath
for Thomas,
this talk of home,
of place prepared
if no Way
is found to reach its gate,
no Truth
that substantiates
promised Life,
when Christ speaks
coming death.

XVIII

New sap engorged,
these eager tendrils chance
across the wall;
stemming from the Branch,
fruit-laced limbs with joy embrace
the ripening glory of life in Him,
the harsh pruning of His grace.

I AM THE TRUE VINE, AND MY FATHER IS THE VINEDRESSER.
[15:1]

XIX

For a little while this labour,
pain's lamented occupation,
surge of quickening contraction
and then
deliverance—
the Son's advent once again,
the gasp of new life
deposing the cry
of scarce remembered struggle.

XX

Making a run for it,
each of you will scatter home,
scuttle away as I sink
in suffering
not yet believing that I am
overcoming by being overcome,
left behind, but not alone.

XXI

They seek Jesus,
through lantern-lit darkness,
over broken garden ground,
steeled and tooled to fell him
if need be; but on hearing his *I AM*
they each fall backwards, to their knees.

XXII

Calloused hands,
war hardened to thorns,
the flourishing cruelties
of iron-bound earth,
plait a barbarous crown,
embed it on the blood-sweated brow
of a smitten King,
before whose shame they bow.

XXIII

His own,
this cross—
although others might have borne
its rude timber at a time—
shouldering the beam, not light,
he lumbers towards the brink,
where laying down
he will be lifted high.

He went out, bearing his own cross, to the place called The Place of a Skull. [19:17]

XXIV

A point put on the words—
to crucify—
to jar and joggle every joint,
upheave unbroken bone,
crush cartilage, nailing every nerve
to die. The gasping Word of God
contracted to a groan.

XXV

His hands new cleansed
Pilate will engrave heaven's King
into a cross;
and though disdaining truth, he still
sets words to work,
openly proclaims a suffering Sovereign,
crushed by his own people's will.

IN   RI

XXVI

These remnants,
final effects of a criminal left alone,
are now divided—like flesh, torn.
Boasting that evening
at the barrack mess
or at hearth,
each will bring a piece of Calvary home.

When the soldiers had crucified Jesus, they took his garments and divided them into four parts. [19:23]

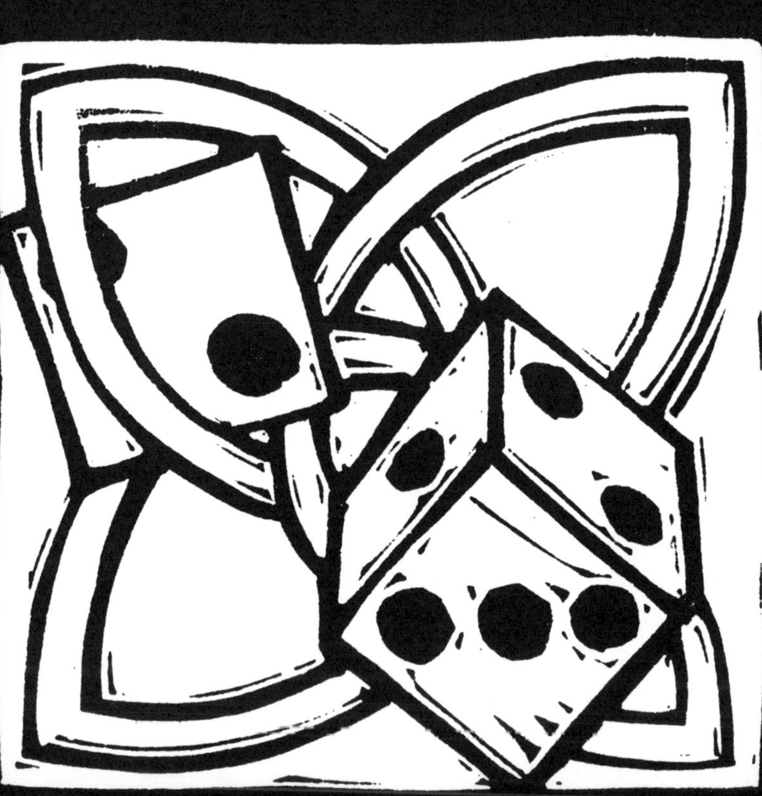

XXVII

His withering tongue—
palate parched—
creaks out encrusted thirst,
and savours sour wine salve,
(the cup drained dry).
Such bitter balm will grace
his arid lips to lisp
the blood-wrought word,
Tetelestai.

XXVIII

Mere carrion, these carcasses now,
the soldiers congregate,
before this central Man.
Finding no more breath in him,
they spare his unbroken bones,
probe his heart,
and saturate
with bloody water
Golgotha's brow.

But one of the soldiers pierced his side with a spear, and at once there came out blood and water. [19:34]

XXIX

In vacant space
they lay him down,
prepare him a place
and him prepare;
bind death in linen cloth,
weeping wounds they dress in myrrh.
With Sabbath's dawning sunset
they leave him there.

So because of the Jewish day of Preparation, since the tomb was close at hand, they laid Jesus there. [19:42]

XXX

Nameless,
this believing man
leans deeper into death's
cast remnants
and, with unscripted heartbeat's trust,
embraces what the Christ could be,
alive
to the breathing possibility
that, he, dying
might rise,
and must.

XXXI

In darkness still,
the grave still darker,
Mary glosses stony absence,
reads aloud a stolen Lord
from the tomb's
mouthing toothless yawn.
Retracing her steps
she recounts
the blank nothing of no dawn.

BUT MARY STOOD WEEPING OUTSIDE THE TOMB, AND AS SHE WEPT SHE STOOPED TO LOOK INTO THE TOMB. [20:11]

XXXII

Lap lulled by lifeless waters,
ill-cast nets bearing no weight,
the fishermen see against
charcoal dawn
the lone figure of the Lord—
come to draw them in again,
and launch them out.

XXXIII

Though all the world a long room lined,
and every shelf with volumes crammed,
though all in fairest minuscule inscribed
—they never could contain the sense
of this eternal Word,
or capture Christ.

I SUPPOSE THE WORLD ITSELF COULD NOT CONTAIN
THE BOOKS THAT WOULD BE WRITTEN. [21:25]

meditations

THE POEMS IN 33 ARE DESIGNED TO STAND ALONE AS ALLUSIVE PIECES, HINTING AND NUDGING US TOWARDS JESUS' REVELATION OF HIMSELF. FOR THOSE WHO WISH TO ENGAGE A LITTLE MORE DEEPLY, OR WHO WOULD LIKE TO USE THE POEMS AS A BASIS FOR FURTHER DEVOTIONAL EXERCISES, THE FOLLOWING MEDITATIONS ARE OFFERED AS WAYS TO PURSUE THE GOSPEL'S MEANING MORE FULLY. IN ORDER TO PRESERVE A SENSE OF DISCOVERY FOR THE READER, I HAVE AVOIDED THE TEMPTATION TO OVERLY EXPLAIN ALL OF THE IMAGERY THE POEMS CONTAIN.

1 [JOHN 1:1–18]: *You Are Here*

For those who fear getting lost forever, there are few words on a map that are more consoling. Our position relative to where we have been and where we are going can help us see the journey through.

John 1 stands like that kind of signpost for the gospel traveler. Our feet are straddling the soil of Old Testament and New Testament, pre-incarnation and incarnation. Jesus' coming into the world locates him for us, and us in him. After centuries of silence, we now have the decisive Word from God about where we truly are, because he is now fully here.

II [JOHN 1:19–51]: *Jesus in Our Place*

Jesus in the Jordan should jar us, rankle our sense of propriety. John's baptism is one of repentance, and the one Man who never had to say sorry for sin enters those waters. This poem takes the allusion to Jesus' baptism and works with the idea of claiming ground. Jesus casts his sandal on the interface between sin and repentance, between alienation and finding our home in his land, between life and death, and emerges from the water ready to set the world alight with his righteous gospel.

III [JOHN 2:1–12]: *Wine to Make the Heart Glad*

Providing wine at a wedding can seem like a trivial trick rather than a miracle, but vinification forms an important part of Jesus' vocabulary about the coming of his Kingdom. He is the Vine, our participation in the cup of wine at Communion draws our senses into contact with the tang of what he has done to redeem us, and the inbreaking of his work is the new wine which splits the seams of old and dead religion. The guests and revellers at Cana were enjoying a foretaste of what Jesus came to provide. As N.T. Wright says, "The transformation from water to wine is of course meant by John to signify the effect that Jesus can have, can still have today, on people's lives."[1]

1   Tom Wright, *John for Everyone, Part 1: Chapters 1–10* (London: Society for Promoting Christian Knowledge, 2014, orig. publ. 2002), p. 22.

IV [JOHN 2:13–25]: *Touching the Temple*

Your readings through John's gospel will bring you face to face with something the author is preoccupied with: *people misunderstanding Jesus.* Whether by his closest disciples or his harshest critics, Jesus was often misconstrued, his nuance lost, the loaded nature of his language overlooked. The Temple talk in John 2 is a classic case of crossed purposes. Jesus is speaking about his death and resurrection, his opponents about designs and construction. This poem plays on this misunderstanding, showing how the dissolution of our true Temple, Jesus, is both tragic and triumphant—a death that will birth new life and new access. In him we have a new meeting place, and a hitherto unimagined intimacy with God.

V [JOHN 3]: *The New Birth*

The new birth that Jesus preaches cannot be reduced to mere mechanics, cannot be caricatured by some pale intellectual understanding of what it means. Nicodemus is a literalist, a dead prose afficionado, a stubborn curator of the possible. Jesus, on the other hand introduces a concept which spells silent revolution, a new creation, a calling of life out of nothing, the Spirit work of bringing people into being through faith in Christ.

VI [JOHN 4]: *Weary for Water*

This poem draws on imagery spread across the Bible about God's
faithful covenant love to us. Jesus' dealings with the Samaritan
woman are tender and true, loving and probing, empathetic and
directive. Her life experiences, either through her own mistakes
or (more likely) her mistreatment by others, renders her in a place
where Jesus' words about lasting refreshment find a ready reception.
In her story we see our story, filled by the one who came to empty
himself for our sake; in the holy company of the one who sees our
brokenness and sin and yet leads us out to life.

VII [JOHN 5]: *Full and Final Theology*

John's gospel is a kind of theological "show and tell" where the visible
works of Jesus speak the invisible realities of who he is and what he
has come to do. Here Jesus speaks in terms which are as expansive
as the universe—he and the Father are one—and as mundane as the
grave. The reality of Jesus' God-incarnated identity, is transgressive
of the man-made boundaries that his contemporaries had placed on
who the Messiah might be, and transformative of all who will come
to him by faith. His life is our light and life, his sheer "god-ness"
the entire grounds on which we rest our hope of resurrection.

VIII [JOHN 6]: *Better Bread*

Ulterior motives abounded on the part of those who trailed around
behind Jesus in Galilee. Some were intrigued and others were
thrilled by the spectacular things that he could do; still others were
opposed to him. The feeding of the 5,000 is both compassion and
connection. Jesus' feels for those who come to hear him teach, but
he also connects his work of bread in the wilderness with God's
provision of manna in the desert. This poem seeks to reflect this,
the deeper and more vivid reality of Jesus given for our sake and
for our satisfaction.

IX [JOHN 7]: *Arrested*

This poem seeks to capture the reversal of fortune experienced on
the part of those charged by the chief priests and Pharisees to appre-
hend Jesus. The deciding factor against Jesus being incarcerated is
not superiority of firepower on his part, or by a security detail which
fences him from opponents—it is his words. No one ever spoke like
he did. He disarms those who carry weapons, and arrests those who
seek to capture, merely by his "word-woven bands." This points to
the power of his speech, but even more so to his person—the *Logos*
revealing and articulating God in new and captivating ways.

X [JOHN 8]: *Nebula*

The imagery in Jesus' words about his place in history and eternity
are breath-taking. John 8:56 finds John's record of Jesus' speech at
a particular highpoint—opening up a channel whereby we can see
Jesus as the Christ, and the one in continuity with God's covenant
promises across the ages. This poem seeks to take Abraham's point
of view, conveying the bedazzlement of looking down history's
ages and seeing, nebulously, the outline of the Deliverer. John joins
Genesis to Jesus, and this poem invites us to do the same.

XI [JOHN 9]: *The Blind Leading the Blind*

In case we become accustomed to miracles, Jesus' work in John 9
presents us with a muddy metaphor, with an action on Jesus' part
that visualized the amazing act of restoring sight to a man. The
blindness John emphasizes in this section of his gospel is chiefly
spiritual. Jesus can make the world flare into light for a man who
was blind from birth, he can restore the world to him and him to the
world, but those who interrogate the miracle betray their own
spiritual unseeing. This poem seeks to nerve the miracle again,
to leave us asking if we have likewise been given sight to behold
Jesus as he truly is.

XII [JOHN 10]: *Violence and Shepherding*

Sometimes our concept of Jesus as our shepherd is too safe. Domesticated by photos of Welsh valleys mantled in green, we tend to think of the Saviour as a bit part actor in a rural scene, a kind of amiable character who feeds and leads. John 10 is much more edgy and violent than that. The shepherd represents the narrow line between chaos and compassion, between destruction and survival, between the warfare of the natural world and the welfare of the flock. Wolves and hired workers stand to either maul or fleece the flock, and so Jesus' work here is muscular and manifestly physical. He is both the point of access to the fold, and the gate which keeps the wolf from the door. Our understanding of his shepherding work must be scented with the potential of blood, with the chest-pounding relief of rescue, and by true safety which sees what could have destroyed us.

XIII [JOHN 11]: *Love's Distance*

The little word *so* in John 11:6 has enough strength to bear the weight of our questions in the midst of grief, and our pain in the seeming absence of the Saviour in times of trouble. This poem seeks to build a tension between Jesus tarrying, and the resurrection he will affect in Bethany. Lazarus' tomb, while surrounded by tears, will be the theatre in which Jesus will play a trailer for his final victory over death, and the final Day when all in him will be raised. The Lord, lingering before going to Bethany, loves his friends in their loss but will tarry so as to bring a better hope than mere sympathizing presence could have conveyed. Such is often our experience, this is always our compassionate Saviour—coming, carrying more comfort than we ever sought at his hand.

XIV [JOHN 12]: *Seeds and Certainty*

In this poem we are confronted not with the physical act of being raised from the dead, but by the theological fact that it represents. Jesus is previewing the pain he will endure at Calvary, preparing the hearts of his followers for the rigors of the cross, for the shame that will snare his heel in coming days. At the heart of this is the simile of seed, the metaphor of sowing and harvesting. Jesus will be humiliated at the cross, but also glorified; destroyed, but also raised. "Harvest-sure" is the key concept in this passage, and in this poem. The laying down of Jesus' life is not merely symbolic but is the concrete guarantee of our share in his risen life, when he comes again. This makes our surrender to him logical, hopeful, and delightful, even though it may entail a cross and loss in the world's eyes.

XV [JOHN 13:1–30]: *Backdrop*

Judas is the tragic reverse image of Jesus. He the self-serving thief, Jesus the self-sacrificing Lord; he the kinsman betrayer, Jesus the kinsman redeemer. We should gasp as Judas leaves the upper room in John 13. His name is so aligned with betrayal that we could minimize his crime. There was nothing in Jesus that could merit betrayal, no wrong deeds that could provide warrant for what Judas does. His act of treachery is of such weight that John's account gives us the most spare details. The night-time which is the backdrop for Judas' betrayal places his act in the kind of tone that the Baroque artist Caravaggio delighted in. Here the heinousness of what Judas does is matched by the spiritual obscurity into which he sinks. His betrayal is reprehensible and salutary, a measure of how far we can turn from the perfections of Jesus, a picture of the dreadful exchange that embracing darkness and rejecting light truly is.

XVI [JOHN 13:31–38]: *Dawning Despair*

There is a kind of poetry in the events leading to Calvary, a sense of time being a story long and beautifully written. The artistry of Jesus' work of salvation is not merely in its physical and spiritual power, but in the ends and means that God weaves so amazingly around this central event in history. Peter's denial, a squalid act of self-preservation, a desperately squirming attempt to avoid the shadow of the cross, is bracketed by a natural world which serves as a chorus for his failure. This poem seeks to capture Peter's pride, and the moment it will be extinguished in the darkness of personal failure. For all of us who stumble, his story is one of hope and help, or restoration and renewal—even if we are broken in that process.

XVII [JOHN 14]: *Believing Thomas*

In church history Thomas has been reduced to a single dimension: *doubt*. Like all of us he is much more than a one-word summary. As a disciple he could believe in spite of the danger (John 11:16) and he would also ask for greater clarity when he couldn't see the way ahead. Like a keen but compliant student, Thomas insists on Jesus expanding on and explaining the poetry of his coming again. Thomas will not be defiant, but he also won't display artificial deference. He wants to *know*, he needs for Jesus to give hope some dimension and direction. As fellow followers, we should be very grateful for Thomas. His is the voice in class asking the questions that burn in our breasts also. The answer he receives from Jesus has built a bridge for all of us to cross, constructed on one foundation, leading us to heaven, knowledge, and true spiritual thriving.

XVIII [JOHN 15]: *Abundant Life*

The *I AM* statements of Jesus are compact poems, atomic truths
which burst into real hope when we probe them. In this poem we
can delight together in the organic and abundant blessing of life with
Christ, and union with him. The imagery of vines and branches has
roots in some of God's earliest promises of deliverance and joy from
him. Living under your vine was an image in ancient Israel of secure
belonging, the Righteous Branch was Isaiah's verdant metaphor of
the Messiah who would come, and the later New Testament will bear
witness to fruit bearing from the Spirit. There is a dance in the vine's
chancing growth, a beauty in watching the evidence of vitality and
deep rootedness bearing fruit. That is true in the natural world, and it
is true in the horticulture of the heart. The end of this poem may seem
to resolve in anti-climax but the grace of pruning invites us to loop
back to the life and fruit that follow seasons of difficulty and grief.

XIX [JOHN 16:1–24]: *Love's Labour*

John 13–17 suspends the believer between Jesus' life and death, and
relies on the tension of a kingdom already come and yet to come. The
privilege of the disciples' internship with Jesus is about to come to an
end, the lines of how they relate to him are about to be redrawn, and

in grace the Saviour explains that absence now is a mere guarantee
of presence later. The imagery Jesus borrows is from childbirth: the
now-centered urgency and agony of labor is eventually lost in the
euphoria of birth and the new life that has finally arrived. So, too,
for the disciples: the reordering of things around the cross is not the
beginning of the end but the end of the beginning, not death throes
but birth pangs. They stand on the threshold of the gospel's sweet
irony—loss that leads to life, death that leads to victory, temporal
absence which guarantees eternal presence. We do not share their
location in history, but the tension is real for us as well.

xx [JOHN 16:25–33]: *Left Behind, but Not Alone*

Imagine two things: you are about to face a horrible trial and every-
one who loves you will forsake you. The people you have invested
love and time in seem to flee with unnerving briskness, with blithe
concern only for their own skins. This is Jesus' prospect in this pas-
sage. The disciples whom he loves, whose feet he has washed, whose
lives he has changed, will all betray him in one way or another—and
he knows it. Jesus confidence in this crisis is that the Father will be
with him, even though Psalm 22 will bruise his soul when wracked
on the cross. This weighty reality, this is the Saviour's dignity, this is
our salvation. Would you bow in worship of him just now?

XXI [JOHN 17–18]: *I AM*

This poem seeks to combine the faltering search of Jesus' enemies
and the felling certainty of who he is. Theirs is the fumbling through
obscurity to arrest the King of Life, his the timeworn, eternity borne
word of who he is—the irreducible certainty of his status as God
the Son. In a simple statement Jesus charges his life and death with
all of the covenant significance of the promises to Abraham and the
counsels of eternity. In the corner of a garden, in a small corner of
the world, Jesus is surrounded by those who will take his life, but
he is likewise established in the reality of who he is. This is no mere
Middle-Eastern skirmish or religious schism—these are the forces of
darkness and light pitted against one another. The sword may seek
to fell Jesus, but his word is enough to repel enemies who are armed
to the teeth. Here the irresistible momentum of eternity is seemingly
arrested by the immovable object of opposition and hatred, but this
"I AM" will pass right through the death they deal him, and carry
many sons and daughters to life in the process.

XXII [JOHN 19:1–15]: *Making War on Jesus*

Consider the soldiers who handle Jesus. They are not movie extras who have waited in the wings for a fleeting cameo in the Bible story. These are war-hardened men, exposed in body and soul to the barbarity of conflict, instruments of the brute force of empire, lock-stepped infantry whose might has rolled the world under Rome's wheels. These men casually deal in death, are muscled and toned by savagery and torture, inured to the shock of blood and broken bone, witnesses to death's trampling march across continents.

Their might is now unleashed on the Messiah. The careless cruelty of men of war is now discharged on Jesus' head, an Empire's power poured upon his solitary brow. His cries and groans will not move them to pity, his lacerated back, his crumbling gait sliding in his own blood and saliva will elicit no compassion.

This is Jesus, our Jesus, beard-plucked, thorn-crowned, blood-baptized, wallowing under the weight of sin's spiked reality.

They will destroy him with fearful expertise, stretch his life like a thin thread across their fine-tuned torture, bring him to the brink and climax of human existence and hold him there—exquisite and excruciating.

This is Jesus, our Jesus. Behold the Man.

XXIII [JOHN 19:16–17]: *His Own, This Cross*

Consider the cross that Jesus carries, and that will carry Jesus. This is neither icon nor emblem, but the used property of every body that ever hung against its crude carpentry. This poem seeks to play on the recycled nature of the cross, on the fact that it was unremarkable in its physical reality. Others had died on this very piece of wood, its grain sapped with blood, its fibers sweat infused.

Jesus dies on a cross he did not own, but that he makes his own. Surely this is the heart of what atonement means, the image of absolute substitution. There is, however, a vital point to grasp here—Jesus will not merely be lifted on the brow of a hill, but is exalted on the brow of the world. His subjugation is his glorification, his trampling by Rome is his triumph over death. "His own, this cross, although others might have borne its rude timber at a time."

XXIV [JOHN 19:18–19]: *Contracted to a Groan*

Charles Wesley masterfully captured the essence of the incarnation in his famous words "Our God contracted to a span." This poem plays on this phrasing, reducing this incarnated one to his groaning on the cross. Ours is an age of anesthetic and medication, of treatment and palliation, and so envisaging the cross is almost impossible to us.

Jesus' body on the cross is a nerve laid bare to all the pain that can be inflicted on it. His whole life now a single agonizing note, a bare minimum of misery, a casting aside of his majesty and dignity which is beyond the comprehension of heart or mind. Take time to think through the crucifixion, recite this poem aloud, and do not release yourself from the horror of what Jesus here endures. His work is glorious, but his pain unbearable. All of this is for you and me.

xxv [JOHN 19:20–22]: *In Two Minds*

Pontius Pilate is the ultimate icon of postmodernism: strident in action but wavering in conviction; ambivalent about meaning but certain in his wording. A governor is in the presence of the King and all he can work through are political ramifications, personal ambitions, kingdom coalitions. Pilate has opportunity to probe Jesus and uncover truth; instead he merely tries him and discards truth.

It is easy to get the upper hand on Pilate, now that Jesus is risen, but we can be likewise political in our animal instincts. We can refuse to climb fully on board with convictions that might implicate us in the inconvenience of a cross, or the derision of a crowd. Pilate is the emblem of our inborn double-mindedness, the Everyman of our hesitation to believe as we ought, for fear of where it might lead. He is despicable and recognizable. See? It is your hands in the bowl.

XXVI [JOHN 19:23–25]: *Reflection: Jesus Trophies*

Somewhere in Palestine in the first century a Roman soldier brought a part of a garment home. One can imagine the scrutinizing gaze of his wife as she weighs its integrity, and calculates either its worth at market or its potential to be worn by a member of the family. These are the mere effects of a criminal, but a nice bonus for a military family to enjoy.

This poem takes Jesus' effects as its starting point, capturing their insignificance in material terms, but also the deeper spiritual reality behind them. No one left Golgotha unscathed. Soldiers returning home had not just been party to one more execution, but were witnesses and culpable participants in the murder of the Son of God. They had willfully and cruelly destroyed the most righteous man who ever lived. The fabric of Jesus' garments would find a home among them, but so too the guilt and trauma of having crucified God.

XXVII [JOHN 19:26–30]: *Internalizing Calvary*

The genre of gospel account does not overly concern itself with the internal life of Jesus. The power and pathos of his story comes to us via the medium of events and outcomes. Occasionally, though, the veil is drawn back and we enter Jesus' world of pain for just a moment. His thirst is one such space.

Jesus is being ravaged by death. The physical and spiritual enormity of his crucifixion are now locked in the eternal present that pain brings with it. He teeters on the edge of death, lingers on the threshold of destruction, and his mouth can barely move for thirst.

This poem takes his thirst as its main image, and seeks to invest it with the cup-draining work of Jesus as Messiah, the bitterness of what he endured, the ripping away of all well-being that the cross achieved. Think of him in his thirst, weep for him here.

XXVIII [JOHN 19:31–37]: *Cadaverous Christ*

The Son of God is now a dead body, the life ripped from it. This poem imagines this moment when Calvary is no longer pain-wracked, when the groans of the Son of God are silent, but when the probing continues. The spearing of Jesus' side is taken here as a symbol of the life that will issue from this ignominious death. The deadness of Jesus in these moments too easily escapes us, the scandal that his resurrection will be too easily evades us. Dead Jesus hangs helpless, lifeless, vanquished, spent. How we ache for his new-buried body to emerge from the grave!

XXIX [JOHN 19:38–40]: *The Space Between*

The space between Jesus' burial and resurrection is easy to ignore. We are readers and we like action; we want to leapfrog from Jesus' defeated body to his victorious body. But John wants us to process what happens in the interim. Here his body is embalmed, the mess of his misery mopped from gaping wounds, his body lifeless, cradled again as in a mother's arms, as death is bound in bandages in anticipation of its bonds being broken. "Sabbath's dawning sunset" is where we are left here, in the trembling twilight between hope's apparent death and death's certain demise.

XXX [JOHN 20:11–31]: *The Disciple Whom Jesus Loved*

There is a humility at the heart of John's account. The man who names protagonists and antagonists, who coins new terms and revives old words, remains nameless to us. Here at the grave's threshold new concepts land in his heart, new faith grips his soul, the dying and rising Jesus now becomes a present and personal reality to him. Unnamed through humility, perhaps, but such

anonymity brings us into contact with him too. We are disciples
whom Jesus loves, we too stand on the verge of resurrection
reality and find the same light dawning in our souls.

XXXI [JOHN 20:1–10]: *The New Language of Resurrection*

The resurrection of Jesus was a retooling of human language and a
reframing of human story. Jesus' resurrection trained the trajectory
of hope away from mere stories of escape from death and on to the
reality of hope through death. This poem uses the image of parsing a
new grammar, standing with Mary as she seeks to make sense of the
absence of Jesus, of the emptiness of the tomb, and with a present
and future which, for her, were as yet unwritten. This moment in
John's gospel invites us into the inkling of what wonder will be when
Jesus is fully witnessed, encourages us to balance grief and hope
between the brute reality of sin's ruin and the suggestive hope of sin
itself being ruined. We will need new words to speak this truth—
Jesus' resurrection will supply them in abundance.

XXXII [JOHN 21:1–19]: *Fishers of People*

The return to his old trade marked a moment of defeat and conviction for Peter. His denial of the Lord seemed to overpower even the transformative work of resurrection in his life. Jesus' appearance at the shore of Galilee firmly communicates that the resurrection will not allow anyone to return to the mere nine-to-five. Jesus' powerful life and defeat of death mean that everything has changed, and that our task, though related to our past occupation, is suffused with the light of the living Lord.

XXXIII [JOHN 21:20–25]: *The End and the Beginning*

John's gospel concludes with a dazzling possibility—the life of Jesus would fill more books than the world could hold. The drama and poetry of this gospel account are designed not to draw a line under Jesus and the gospel but to invite us into a story and reality which will encompass us, our world, and all of eternity. John's gospel ends not with a full-stop (or period), but with an ellipsis—with the ever powerful reality that Jesus is alive, that he cannot now be reduced to a concept or a mere moment in history. He is risen, he is Lord, he is our Saviour and our hope.

ANDREW ROYCROFT is a pastor and poet from Northern Ireland. His poetry has been published in various literary journals including *Honest Ulsterman* and *The North*, and has regularly been featured on The Rabbit Room. Poems by Andrew have been read on BBC radio, used in collaboration with community arts projects, and in partnership with New Irish Arts. A medievalist by background, his interests include ministry, theology, literature, culture, travel, and the natural world. Andrew has held a variety of pastorates in Northern Ireland as well as having served in Perú for a short period in missions work. He also serves as a visiting lecturer in Biblical Theology at the Irish Baptist College. Andrew is husband to Carolyn, and dad to Grace and Hannah. Together they live in Co. Armagh with a multitude of pets.

MALCOLM GUITE is an English poet, singer-songwriter, Anglican priest, and academic. Guite is the author of multiple books of poetry and several books on Christian faith and theology, his most recent being *Lifting the Veil: Imagination and the Kingdom of God.*

NED BUSTARD is a graphic designer, children's book illustrator, author, and printmaker. Some of his books include *Revealed: A Storybook Bible for Grown-Ups, It Was Good: Making Art to the Glory of God, The Lost Tales of Sir Galahad,* and *Saint Patrick the Forgiver.*

3 more books to help reflect on the bible

How To See: Reading God's Word with New Eyes
A.D. Bauer offers tools of interpretation that can help us observe important details in the Bible, enabling us to see God's Word with new eyes.

Lifting the Veil: Imagination and the Kingdom of God
In this book, poet Malcolm Guite explores how the creative work of poets and other artists can kindle our imaginations for Christ.

Revealed: A Storybook Bible for Grown-Ups
Revealed offers gripping artwork—from medieval woodcuts to contemporary linocuts—depicting well-known passages along with those shocking stories that are often hidden from view.

squarehalobooks.com